BRITISH RAILWAYS

PAST and PRESENT

No 25

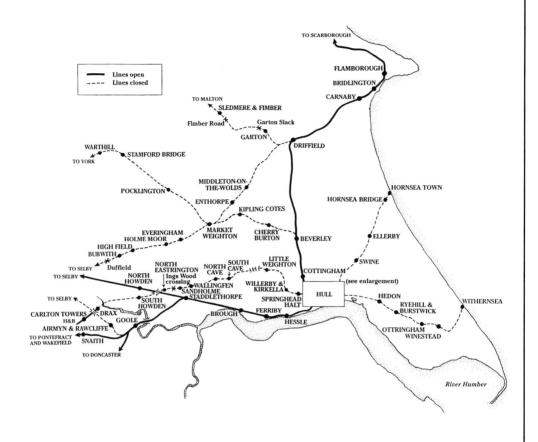

BRITISH RAILWAYS

PAST and PRESENT

No 25

East Yorkshire

Roger Hill & Carey Vessey

Past and Present

Past & Present Publishing Ltd

To Alexandra, Victoria, Jade and Autumn

© Roger Hill & Carey Vessey 1995

First published in 1995
Reprinted 1999
Reprinted 2003

British Library Cataloguing in Publication Data

A catalogue record for this book is available from the British Library

ISBN 1 85895 079 1

Past & Present Publishing Ltd
The Trundle
Ringstead Road
Great Addington
Kettering
Northants
NN14 4BW

Tel/Fax: 01536 330588
email: sales@nostalgiacollection.com
Website: www.nostalgiacollection.com

Printed and bound in Great Britain

GARTON SLACK CROSSING: An unusual view from the brake-van of the twice-weekly 10.10 Malton-Market Weighton-Selby pick-up freight (also seen on page 157) on 25 September 1958 headed by 'J39' 0-6-0 No 64928. The guard is opening the gates to the road after the passage of the train. These days it is difficult to imagine that the seemingly minor road is in fact the main A166 from York to Bridlington.

In summer 1994 the A166 at this point is wider and considerably busier. The trackbed is marked by the row of trees on the left and the location can be identified from the background hills and trees. *Tony Ross/RKH*

CONTENTS

HULL, BOTANIC GARDENS: A superb view of Botanic Gardens station in about 1959 with an eight-car Birmingham DMU set bound for Hornsea passing a short pick-up freight headed by a tender-first LMS Class '4' 'Mogul'. Note the trolleybus wires.

Botanic Gardens was one of Hull's infamous level crossings, but this time one that a certain Dr Beeching disposed of in the early 1960s at no expense to the local authority. For many years the station site was a builders' yard, but a new public house has now been built there, opened in November 1994. Messrs Fairburn are still in business, although not from this building, which remains as a listed structure. *N. E. Stead/RKH*

INTRODUCTION

'Change' - this one word most closely describes the contents of this book. Regrettably, although some rolling-stock is better, there are no examples of improvements to the railway infrastructure in an area that is geographically so extensive. Approximately half the lines have closed completely, and even the former busy railway 'crossroads' at Market Weighton is now devoid of track.

It has often been stated, even in official quarters, that with hindsight the closure of the direct Hull-York route was a grave error, with a local service to Hedon (along the Withernsea line) coming a close second for crassness. It is only through suffering the vagaries of the local roads, particularly during rush-hour periods, that these comments can be fully appreciated.

The routes covered in this volume range from the industrial through rural to coastal, with the pictures hopefully reflecting them all. We have given much thought to the contents, eventually concluding that owing to pressure of space and lack of suitable vintage material, oddities such as the Spurn Head Railway have had to be omitted.

Starting from the west this book deals first with the Goole area, moving on to the lines to Hull from Goole and Selby and the Hull & Barnsley line, which naturally leads to Hull itself. To the east, the Holderness branches to Hornsea and Withernsea are looked at, followed by Beverley and the line to the Yorkshire coast. The final part encompasses the lines through the Wolds, York to Beverley and Selby to Driffield and Malton, both via Market Weighton.

Authors' licence has been exercised to extend beyond boundaries where something of note could be shown, and which has not been portrayed elsewhere in the series. Some locations entailed much planning and time being spent on them, while others were secured more simply and almost by chance. The compilation of this work has given two men from very different backgrounds much enjoyment and often amusement. It is with these pleasures that the book has been compiled and is hopefully read, giving some insight into the area's railways, as well as a flavour of their past.

In conclusion it would be remiss not to express our gratitude for the help received from many photographic contributors, as well as from railway staff and other people not connected with the railways at all. We would particularly like to thank Associated British Ports - Peter Cook and Colin Silvester - for access to Hull and Goole Docks respectively, Alan Thompson and Ernie Sunderland for their sterling work in the darkroom, Kevin Headon at Trans-European Port Services, Lynne White and Sally McKone for transcript work, various learned members of the RCTS for their valuable advice, and finally our long-suffering wives Jean and Lesley for their forbearance.

Roger Hill
Carey Vessey

The Goole area

The first railway to reach the inland port of Goole was the Wakefield, Pontefract & Goole (later part of the Lancashire & Yorkshire) in 1848. The North Eastern link from Gilberdyke (Staddlethorpe) Junction to Doncaster opened in 1869. The L&Y and the Gilberdyke-Goole sections have been the subjects of closure speculation in recent years, but both still survive. A third line in the area, the Isle of Axholme Joint, is covered in the Lincolnshire volume.

GOOLE (1): Local 'B1' 4-6-0 No 61215 *William Henton Carver* pauses at Goole with a heavy King's Cross-Hull train on 13 April 1961.

A Class '156' 'Sprinter' bound for Hull is seen at the same spot in spring 1994. The wooden platform extensions and the footbridge were declared unsafe and removed in 1992 and 1993 respectively, as a result of which the HST service to and from King's Cross can no longer stop at Goole as the remaining platforms are too short. Can this be progress? *P. Cookson/RKH*

GOOLE (2): BR Standard Class '3' 2-6-0 No 77001 pulls into the up platform at Goole with the 16.30 local service for Wakefield on 1 June 1957. Several of these elusive 'Moguls' were allocated to the Hull area in the late 1950s.

Apart from the demolition of the goods shed and the removal of the platform extensions, very little has altered in July 1994 as a Regional Railways-liveried Class '144' unit arrives forming a Hull-Doncaster service. *H. C. Casserley/RKH*

GOOLE (3): Gresley 'V3' 2-6-2T No 67635 leaves Goole with the Hull portion of the up 'Yorkshire Pullman' on 13 April 1961. The four cars will combine with the main train at Doncaster. This luxury service (latterly as the 'Hull Pullman' and the 'Hull Executive') continued until the advent of HSTs, and was one of, if not the, last regular 'Deltic' workings.

What is now the only through weekday service between Hull and King's Cross, the 07.05 from Hull, is seen from the same footbridge in June 1994.

P. Cookson/RKH

11

GOOLE (4): Ex-Great Central 'O4/3' 2-8-0 No 63845 trundles a brake-van across Boothferry Road crossing and approaches Goole station on 13 April 1961. Apart from the signalling little has changed in the spring of 1994 as a Class '141' 'Pacer' unit bound for Hull crosses the same level crossing, a constant source of annoyance to road users in Goole that at busy times cuts the town in half. *P. Cookson/RKH*

GOOLE MPD: As many shed-bashers of the time will remember, the Lancashire & Yorkshire shed at Goole was one of the most isolated and difficult to reach in the country, being at least 30 minutes' walk from the station, and with no road access. Here is the shed on 13 April 1961 with an unusual visitor, Gresley 'J39' 0-6-0 No 64749, by the coaling plant, and in the background several of the ubiquitous 'WD' 2-8-0s with which the area abounded.

The shed was closed in 1967 and subsequently completely demolished. However, the site, being so isolated, was left derelict, and in 1990 the Humberside Locomotive Preservation Group proposed to transfer its headquarters there from Hull Dairycoates. Unfortunately the plan fell through, but not before the Group had excavated all the inspection pits. The shed road pits are shown in spring 1994 in the third picture, and the spot from which Peter Cookson's picture was taken was plotted by reference to the excavated water tower inspection pit, which is immediately behind the mound of earth in the left-centre of the second picture. *P. Cookson/ RKH (2)*

GOOLE DOCKS (1) were served by a maze of tracks, and for many years were shunted by a small stud of ex-L&Y saddle tanks allocated to Goole. Here 0-4-0ST Nos 51222 and 51244 take a breather on the lines leading to Railway Dock on 9 June 1960. Within a year the two tanks, together with local sister No 51241, had gone for scrap.

Rails do still exist in the undergrowth in 1994, although they will never carry a train again. Several lineside buildings and of course the church remain, but the gasworks has disappeared. *P. Cookson/RKH*

GOOLE DOCKS (2): The crew of No 51222 pose having just crossed Bridge Street level crossing in 1960. At the same spot in spring 1994 the rails, level crossing and footbridge have gone, but the building on the left remains. *P. Cookson/RKH*

GOOLE DOCKS (3): Coming out of Ship Dock on 7 June 1960 is No 51244 with a couple of wagons. The same location in 1994 is a dock roadway, the old buildings have vanished and containers are everywhere.
P. Cookson/RKH

GOOLE DOCKS (4): Following on from the previous picture, No 51244 crosses Bridge Street and heads for the L&Y goods yard, as local docker Mr George Huntington looks quizzically at the photographer.

Mr Huntington has sadly passed away and rails no longer cross Bridge Street at this point, either at or (in the distance) above ground level. However, Number 19 Shed on the right still stands, as does the flat-roofed cafe. *P. Cookson/RKH*

GOOLE DOCKS (5): No 51244 and one of the ex-L&Y 0-6-0STs, No 51521, shunt the busy docks near Bridge Street on 21 April 1956.

Tracks still exist at this location in 1994, as do the water towers (known locally as the 'Salt and Pepper Pot'), and in the bushes can be found the base of the lamp standard to the left of No 51521's smokebox. Recently (October 1994) rail traffic has returned to these yards in the form of a load of Renault cars imported through the Channel Tunnel and off-loaded at Goole to be distributed throughout the country by road. *N. E. Stead/RKH*

AIRMYN & RAWCLIFFE: The branch from Goole to Selby was opened in 1912 and closed in 1964. A Birmingham RC&W DMU forming a Goole-Selby service runs into this entirely wooden station on 6 July 1964.

The station site is now part of a garden whose owner kindly allowed access for the picture to be taken. The trackbed can be seen curving away to the right in the distance, and behind the photographer towards Selby it now forms part of a new relief road connecting the M62 motorway with Drax Power Station. The road bridge was not demolished until 1993. *D. P. Leckonby/RKH*

SNAITH station, on the L&Y line between Goole, Pontefract and Wakefield, is seen in the 1950s with a freight comprised largely of cattle wagons and headed by LMS Class '2' 2-6-0 No 46487.

By the summer of 1994 the line has been singled and clings to life by a thread. Freight services have long ceased and the three passenger trains per weekday are formed of 'Pacer' units. *J. W. Armstrong/RKH*

The North Eastern main line

The first railway into Hull was the Hull & Selby Railway, opened on 1 July 1840, which subsequently became part of the North Eastern and which is now (with the Doncaster-Goole link which joins at Gilberdyke) the main trunk route serving the city.

NORTH HOWDEN: BR Standard Class '5' 4-6-0 No 73141 returns an excursion from the coast through Howden (renamed from North Howden in 1961) on 8 August 1967.

   Vanity insisted that Howden Station be included since it is the home of one of the authors, Roger Hill, whose wife and granddaughter watch the passage of the VSOE Pullman set headed by Class '47' No 47630 on 3 April 1994. *Doug Hardy/RKH*

STADDLETHORPE (1): Here the main line was four-track from 1904 until reduced to two in 1989. Seen from the road bridge in May 1961 is a Gresley 'K3' 2-6-0 standing in the platform road, and sister engine No 61935 with a fish train on the up fast, signalled towards Goole. Fish trains were once a common sight, but ceased in the mid-1960s and the majority of fish traded through Hull is now transported by road.

In 1974 the station became known as Gilberdyke Junction, and the second view from the same spot in January 1983 shows Class '46' No 46045 facing the wrong way on the down relief road with an engineers train. Note that the siding behind the up platform has been extended into a full loop.

In the third view another engineers train, headed by Class '47' No 47319, runs through the up platform, signalled for the Goole line, in November 1994. As with other stations on this section, the platforms were extended outwards when the relief roads were lifted in 1989. *B. Todd/A. Dibnah/RKH*

STADDLETHORPE (2): Seen from the road bridge, and looking in the opposite direction, 'K3' No 61883 brings a long mixed freight from the Selby direction on to the down relief road in June 1961, with the line from Goole trailing in from the left. The 'K3s' were a common sight in the Hull area for more than 30 years.

Freight trains into Hull in the 1990s are few and far between, but one regular service is the Rylstone Tilcon Aggregates train, seen passing the renamed signal box behind Class '60' No 60095 in March 1993. The record books state that the 18-mile section between Ferriby and Barlby Junction (Selby) is the longest continuous section of straight track in Britain. These photographs show that it is only the *down* line that can claim this distinction! *B. Todd/RKH*

BROUGH (1): The station on 2 August 1961, with 'B1' No 61122 running through with the 08.30 Doncaster-Bridlington, passing the 08.21 Leeds-Hull DMU in the down relief platform.

That platform through line is now part of the station car park, and the old buildings have been replaced with more modern structures. In August 1994 a Leeds-Hull service formed of a Class '142' unit arrives at the station.
Peter Rose/RKH

BROUGH (2): In this view of the station from the east on 9 July 1963 we can see that it had four platforms, all of which are occupied in this view. LMS Class '4' 2-6-0 No 43069 is working the 17.15 Brough-Hull fast and 'V3' No 67638 is on a slow train due to depart at the same time. There are DMUs in both the up platforms and even another in the goods yard.

The same location in August 1994 sees a Class '158' unit forming a Manchester-Hull service leaving the station and a track-tamping machine standing in what remains of the up relief platform. *Peter Rose/RKH*

FERRIBY station in March 1962, with 'J39' No 64709 trundling a pick-up freight along the down relief road, and rapidly being overtaken by a 'K3' with a cement train on the down fast.

The down relief road has since been lifted and that platform extended outwards, but the attractive 1904 buildings remain as the modern equivalent of the 'K3' and its train, the Tilcon Aggregates service, headed by Class '60' No 60068, passes on 14 June 1994. *B. Todd/CV*

HESSLE (1): There was a chalk quarry a mile or so to the west of Hessle that provided large quantities of chalk for a cement works at Wilmington, east of Hull. The uncrushed chalk was brought from the quarry to a crushing plant alongside the main line by a short private standard-gauge steam-operated railway, from where it was transferred into main-line wagons for tripping to Wilmington. 'V2' 2-6-2 No 60886 passes the crushing plant with a loaded fish train bound for Scotland on 27 July 1964.

The quarry had closed and the crushing plant and quarry railway were completely demolished by the late 1970s. Here the 16.35 (Sundays only) Hull-King's Cross HST passes the site of the crushing plant exactly 30 years later in July 1994. The background is now dominated by the Humber Bridge. *Doug Hardy/CV*

HESSLE (2): Approaching Hessle station on 10 October 1964 is local 'B1' No 61032 *Stembok* returning light engine to Hull after delivering a load of empty wagons to the Hessle crushing plant. The Hull area trip locos carried 'J' reporting numbers, and the diagram covering trip J07 sometimes included this working.

On 8 May 1994 a light Class '37', No 37235, passes the same spot on its way to Saltend Refinery to collect the Sunday afternoon Saltend-Mostyn tank train. Behind the fence to the left is the A63 Clive Sullivan Way relief road; the road bridge has been rebuilt to incorporate a crossing of the main road and the Humber Bridge again dominates the background. The house on the hillside is still visible in the trees. *John Foreman/RKH*

HESSLE (3): Seen from the original road bridge, 'WD' 2-8-0 No 90009 moves a cement train out of Hessle yard on to the up relief line on 23 June 1966. No 90009 was one of the last two BR steam locos to be allocated to Hull (the other being No 61306), and was transferred away from Dairycoates to Sunderland on 25 June 1967.

The same location on the evening of 19 June 1994 sees Class '60' No 60070 returning from Hull with the Tilcon Aggregates empties. There are now only two running lines at this point and the goods yard area has been completely taken over by Clive Sullivan Way. The timing of this train is particularly erratic, and the authors had to wait a combined total of seven hours to secure this picture. *Doug Hardy/RKH*

HESSLE (4): In July 1961 a 'WD' heads a Hessle Quarry-Wilmington chalk train; with so much local trip work, tender-first running was commonplace.

The Tilcon Aggregates train passes Hessle in June 1994 with Class '60' No 60067. The platforms have been widened, the signal box has disappeared (signalling now being controlled from Melton Lane to the west and Hessle Road to the east) and the awning roof has been removed to reveal the original handsome buildings beneath. *Mike Lake/CV*

HESSLE HAVEN is just to the east of Hessle station; this is where the Hull railway system strictly begins, and where between 1935 and 1974 the entrance to the Inward Goods Yard was situated, seen behind the engine and first coach. 'D49/2' 4-4-0 No 62775 *The Tynedale* passes Hessle Gasworks and crosses from the fast to the relief road with a Hull-Leeds stopping train in 1958.

Thirty-six years on, Clive Sullivan Way occupies the site of the gasworks, but the railwaymen's cottages and the fast lines survive. Class '60' No 60095 heads the up Tilcon Aggregates empties in the summer of 1994. *B. Todd/CV*

The Hull & Barnsley line

It is well known that the Hull & Barnsley Railway proper never actually reached Barnsley, although it most definitely reached Hull, opening in 1885. It was always primarily a freight line, passenger traffic west of South Howden being withdrawn in 1932 and east of there in 1955. The line west of Springbank in Hull was completely closed between 1959 and 1964, although the high-level line between Hessle Road Junction (Hull) and King George Dock is still in use for Saltend Refinery and occasional other freight traffic.

CARLTON TOWERS: Although strictly in North Yorkshire, this location is included as it is on the only section of the Hull & Barnsley proper west of Hull that still carries rail traffic. Here is the station on 12 May 1957 during a photo-stop by the RCTS 'East Midlander' railtour headed by a rare visitor to the area, 'D16/3' 4-4-0 No 62571.

The section between Hensall and Drax, through Carlton Towers, was re-opened in 1972 to serve Drax Power Station. On August Bank Holiday 1994 Class '56' No 56074 passes with a Drax merry-go-round train. The station buildings are in use as offices and the goods shed on the right has been attractively converted into a private dwelling. *J. F. Oxley/RKH*

SOUTH HOWDEN (1) was the westward extremity of the passenger service between 1932 and 1955, the service being worked for many years by push-pull-fitted ex-North Eastern 'G5' 0-4-4Ts. The normal method of working was to propel from Hull to Howden, cross over and work back bunker-first. Seen from the road bridge, 'G5' No 67253 awaits departure for Hull on 16 April 1955.

The station site is now occupied by housing, although the platforms are not too far below the surface, as the author's friend Jim Blake found when he dug a fishpond in his back garden! The road bridge from which the 'past' picture was taken was demolished in 1980, and thanks are due to local farmer Peter Kealey for the loan of his hydraulic baling trailer and tall stepladder to gain the height. *J. F. Sedgwick/RKH*

37

SOUTH HOWDEN (2): A Hull-South Howden service arrives at the 'terminus' propelled by a 'G5' in the early 1950s.

Steam returns to the Hull & Barnsley in August 1994 as Nigel Crisp prepares his 1930 Wallis & Stevens road-roller for a journey to Pickering. The road bridge has been demolished and the trackbed beyond and through the gate is now the driveway of Howden School. With thanks to Mr & Mrs J. Blake for allowing access to their garden. *J. W. Armstrong/RKH*

NORTH EASTRINGTON WEST: 'WD' No 90571 rumbles over the level crossing with a Hull-bound freight on 31 July 1955.

A distinctive new house is in the process of construction across the trackbed in August 1994. From the back of the house the formation stretches away into the distance. *J. F. Sedgwick/RKH*

INGS WOOD crossing on the last day of passenger service, 31 July 1955, with 'G5' No 67280 working the 14.25 South Howden-Hull service. The house and buildings remain in August 1994, but lorries have taken over the freight traffic from the 'WDs'. *J. F. Sedgwick/RKH*

SANDHOLME: 'WD' No 90704 passes the station on 28 March 1959. Sandholme boasted a large goods yard where in more prosperous times mineral trains would change engines.

The station house lay derelict for many years, but in 1994 was nearing the end of an extensive renovation. The goods yard has been taken over by a caravan company. *N. E. Stead/RKH*

WALLINGFEN: 'WD' No 90704 again, this time with a wood train crossing the Market Weighton canal at Wallingfen on 28 April 1959.

A little over 2 miles of the H&B trackbed between Sandholme and Stonycarr and including the bridge over the canal now forms part of the M62 motorway, which is clear of traffic on a Sunday morning in the summer of 1994. The roof of the house in the centre of the 1959 picture is just visible above the new bridge. *N. Wright collection/RKH*

NORTH CAVE was one of several high-level stations on the H&B where the line ran on an embankment with the platform alongside the first floor. A 'G5' calls with a Hull train in the early 1950s.

The station house survives as one of the finest buildings of its kind in the area. The gable end with its original windows and ornate chimney stack is shown in the matching second view, and the third side view shows the first floor level at which trains ran and (fifth from the left) the doorway through which passengers gained access to the platform. With thanks to Mr & Mrs J. Good for allowing access to their premises. *J. W. Armstrong/RKH*

SOUTH CAVE: 'WD' No 90322 attacks the 1 in 150 rising grade through South Cave with a coal train for Hull in 1957. The view from the same road bridge in spring 1994 shows the restored station house and the remains of the platforms beyond, with the gardens that have taken over the remainder of the trackbed.
Tony Ross/RKH

SUGAR LOAF TUNNEL: Three tunnels were necessary to take the H&B under the Wolds between South Cave and Little Weighton. 'G5' No 67280 propels a Hull-South Howden train down the 1 in 150 grade out of the 132-yard Sugar Loaf Tunnel on 28 March 1955. Apart from the removal of the track, very little has changed in early 1994. Sections of the trackbed are now country walks, especially fascinating for the railway historian. *J. F. Oxley/RKH*

LITTLE WEIGHTON (1): A delightful study of 'G5' No 67337 at Little Weighton in November 1954, with the 11.45 Hull-South Howden service. Note that the train is longer than usual and is not being push-pull worked, hence the engine is working chimney-first.

Little Weighton is another of the H&B stations still largely intact, as seen here in March 1993. Even the wooden shelter on the up platform survives. *J. F. Oxley/RKH*

LITTLE WEIGHTON (2): Another view of the station from the road bridge on 30 July 1955, with No 67337 once again, this time on a Hull train. A beautiful portrait of a country station with even a few passengers in evidence.

The same view in March 1993. Shortly after this date an ominous estate agent's board advertising building plots for sale appeared at the end of the station access road, but fortunately this has now gone and the station building seems to be in the process of renovation. *J. F. Sedgwick/RKH*

LITTLE WEIGHTON (3): 'WD' No 90623 heads a coal train towards Hull through the deep chalk cutting to the east of Little Weighton station on 2 September 1957.

In the summer of 1994 the cutting is much the same, save for the removal of the bridge. The trackbed is a roadway used by lorries serving the quarry that has taken over the line to the west of Little Weighton station. *D. R. Smith/RKH*

WILLERBY & KIRKELLA (1), another of the high-level stations, plays host to the now-preserved 'B1' No 61306 (a Hull celebrity for virtually all its BR life) on an up pick-up freight, probably bound for Little Weighton, in the early 1960s.

The station site is now a complex of flats, but note the old police station building to the right of the block, the roof and chimney of which can be seen just to the left of the station nameboard in the old picture. *N. Wright collection/RKH*

WILLERBY & KIRKELLA (2): This most interesting picture taken by the late Mr J. Wright on 18 August 1968 shows the foundations of the high-level station and (nearest the camera) the supports for the bridge over the road in the course of demolition, with the derelict signal box beyond in the distance.

The present flats complex is seen from the same viewpoint in summer 1994. A section of the old embankment still exists as a public footpath behind the photographer. *J. Wright/RKH*

SPRINGHEAD HALT, opened in 1929 for the commencement of a Sentinel steam railcar service on the H&B, must have been a contender for the title of Britain's smallest station. 'G5' No 67282 arrives with the 12.20 Hull-North Cave on 18 February 1955. The engine would normally have been propelling the train, but is facing right way round because of the horse-box being conveyed immediately behind the engine.

The embankment at the site of the Halt has been removed to make way for a housing development and a tall(ish) ladder was used to gain the maximum safe height to take the 'present' picture in spring 1994. The embankment over which the 'G5' is approaching in the old picture can be seen at the rear of the house. *J. F. Oxley/CV*

HULL CANNON STREET: The original passenger terminus of the H&B was at Cannon Street, close to the city centre, but this was closed to passenger traffic in 1924 following the opening of a spur between Springbank North and Walton Street, connecting the H&B and North Eastern lines and allowing H&B passenger trains to run into Paragon station. Cannon Street, however, remained open for freight until 1968, and 'WD' No 90009 is seen there on 23 June 1965, about to depart with a trip working of coal empties for Inward Yard.

An incredible mass of pallets, containers and other materials (including a couple of covered van bodies on the right) occupies the site of Cannon Street station in summer 1994. The warehouse on the right and the building behind serve to identify the location. *C. H. A. Townley/CV*

The railways of Hull

PARAGON (1): The magnificent terminus station at Hull Paragon was designed by G. T. Andrews for the York & North Midland Railway and opened on 8 May 1848. 'B1' No 61035 *Pronghorn*, probably on an evening Leeds train, simmers in platform 7 on 26 September 1954, alongside a classic ex-Great Central wooden-bodied Kitchen Car.

The same viewpoint in March 1993 reveals that platform 7 is now platform 4, and is occupied by a 'Sprinter'. The modern equivalent of the Kitchen Car is an HST buffet; somehow the food from the Kitchen Car sounds more appealing. *J. F. Oxley/RKH*

PARAGON (2): In this view from the well-known vantage point of Park Street bridge in the early 1960s, five of the 14 platforms appear to be occupied, and 'V3' No 67686 is departing with the 16.25 stopping train to Brough.
In the summer of 1994 the number of rail-served platforms has contracted to 11, and most of the canopies outside the overall roof have disappeared. Fortunately, however, the majority remains intact and is a listed structure. A 'Sprinter' leaves for Bridlington and the 16.35 (Sundays only) through HST service to King's Cross awaits departure. *D. P. Leckonby/RKH*

57

PARAGON (3): This view of the sidings and coal drops on the north side of Paragon yard on 30 January 1966 shows local celebrity 'B1' No 61306 marshalling coaching stock. The 1994 view graphically illustrates the contraction of the railway that has taken place over the intervening 28 years. *Doug Hardy/RKH*

PARAGON (4): Seen from Park Street bridge 'D49/1' No 62720 *Cambridgeshire* runs into Paragon with a train from Bridlington on 18 March 1955.

A combination of Class '156' 'Sprinter' and '144' 'Pacer' units, forming a modern incoming Bridlington service, is seen from the same spot in the summer of 1994. Apart from the buildings on the right, the surrounding landscape has totally altered. *J. F. Oxley/RKH*

WEST PARADE JUNCTION: 'B16/2' 4-6-0 No 61437 heads the 11.50 Hull-Market Weighton-York parcels out of Paragon and under Argyle Street bridge on 16 September 1961. Note the DMU washing plant installed in the late 1950s. The tracks on the right are the main lines to Selby, Leeds and Doncaster and will diverge from the Beverley and coast lines at West Parade box, just under the bridge.

The same viewpoint in summer 1994 sees a Class '142' 'Pacer' forming a Bridlington service. The original washing plant has disappeared, but its successors remain and are still occasionally used. *D. P. Leckonby/RKH*

61

ANLABY ROAD CROSSING: The City of Hull originally contained no fewer than 22 level crossings, which from very early times, long before the advent of the motor vehicle, were recognised as being seriously disruptive to road traffic. Replacement of the crossings by bridges had begun with Park Street (immediately outside Paragon station) in 1871, but by the end of the Second World War there were still 16 in use. After Hessle Road the most troublesome of these was Anlaby Road, which a survey in the mid-1950s showed was closed to road traffic for an average of 3 hours 40 minutes every weekday. On 9 June 1961 'B1' No 61215 *William Henton Carver* negotiates the crossing with a King's Cross-Hull train. Note the Hull Corporation AEC Regent bus in the characteristic blue and white livery of the period.

The crossing was bridged by a road flyover and closed on 31 July 1964. The short sections of the former Anlaby Road at each side of the railway, with the buildings behind, still exist in July 1994 as a Class '158' unit passes forming a Manchester-Hull service. The picture was taken from one of the concrete supports of the road flyover. *Peter Rose/RKH*

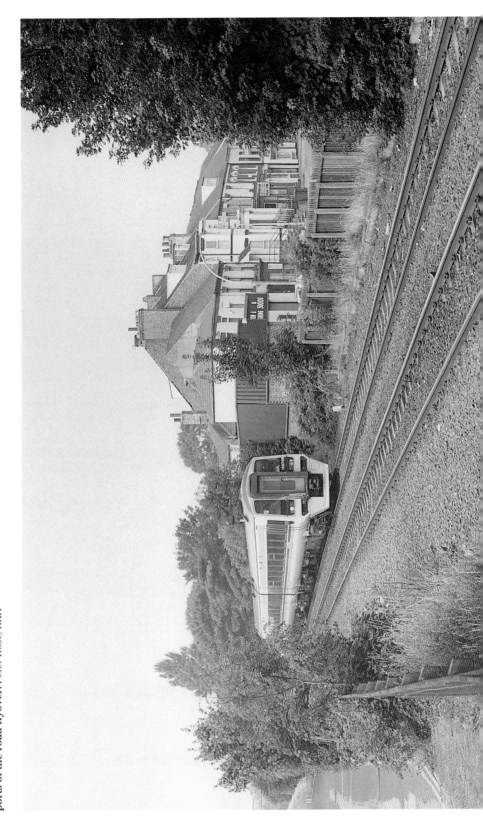

SELBY STREET: Between Anlaby Road and Hessle Road junctions the North Eastern main line to Selby and Doncaster runs parallel with Selby Street. 'V3' No 67684 heads the 16.08 stopping train to Brough on 18 April 1963.

The demolition of the Victorian terraced housing makes the same inner-city location look positively rural by spring 1994 as the 16.35 (Sundays only) Hull-King's Cross HST accelerates away from Paragon. *W. B. Yeadon collection/CV*

HESSLE ROAD JUNCTION (1): The most notorious of the level crossings was at Hessle Road, which the same 1950s survey showed was closed to road traffic between 07.00 and 23.00 on an average weekday on 130 occasions for a total of 6 hours. It was used by all rail traffic out of Paragon to the south, by the direct avoiding line to Beverley and the coast (the Newington branch) and by countless local freight workings. It was crossed by an iron girder bridge carrying the H&B high-level goods lines to Neptune Street goods depot and the docks. On 11 April 1960 the 09.12 Hull-Sheffield (Midland) formed of a four-car Birmingham RC&W DMU passes under the H&B bridge, with Hessle Road Crossing box and the crossing itself in the background.

A 1994 Hull-Sheffield service formed of a Class '156' 'Sprinter' is seen at the same location. Note the road flyover which, with Hessle Road power box, opened in September 1962. This box now controls all rail traffic from Melton Lane (near Ferriby) to Beverley. A link with the past is a remaining section of the former H&B Neptune Street line embankment on the right. *Mike Lake/CV*

HESSLE ROAD JUNCTION (2): In order to construct the Hessle Road flyover, it was necessary to divert the H&B line and to remove the girder bridge. This was achieved by constructing a line down from the high level to join the main lines at Hessle Road Junction at roughly the point of the old level crossing. The diversion is seen on the left of this view of LMS 'Jubilee' 4-6-0 No 45694 *Bellerophon* approaching the junction with a Bridlington-Bradford return excursion on 25 July 1964. The train has taken the Newington branch from Cottingham South Junction in order to avoid reversal at Paragon, which is served by the lines to the right. It was a tolerant house-wife who hung out her clean sheets to dry in this environment!

The access to the high-level line, via Boothferry Park and Springbank South, has been much simplified, and the Newington Branch was abandoned (thus achieving the abolition of a further three level crossings) on the opening of the Anlaby Road curve in 1965. The site of the branch at this point has been taken over by housing development and the houses on the right have been replaced by industrial buildings. Class '47' No 47762 returns from Scarborough with a Pathfinder railtour to Bristol on 30 July 1994. *Peter Rose/Peter Millar*

NEWINGTON signal box controlled the level crossing with Anlaby Road on the Hessle Road Junction-Cottingham South Junction (Newington) branch. Dairycoates 'K3' No 61819 heads north over the crossing with a Bridlington-bound excursion comprised of LMS stock in 1960. Note the trolleybus wires.

The trackbed has been taken over by the inevitable DIY Superstore, but the old tram/trolleybus depot on the left remains. *D. P. Leckonby/CV*

WATERWORKS CROSSING was the next level crossing to the north of Newington, where the line crossed Springbank. The signalman is opening the gates to road traffic in mid-1960 after the passage of Standard Class '3' No 77012 heading south with an Inspection Saloon. The picture was taken from the overbridge carrying the H&B high-level line.

The same vantage point in spring 1994 shows the trackbed converted into a public footpath, which stretches from Anlaby Road to the site of Cottingham South Junction, where the Newington branch joined the Paragon-Beverley line. *N. E. Stead/CV*

COTTINGHAM SOUTH JUNCTION on 10 September 1959 with 'V3' No 67640 heading the 13.20 Hull-Scarborough local. The Newington branch diverges to the right, where ex-L&Y 0-6-0 No 52319 from Goole depot can be seen waiting on the up road with a brake-van.

The elevation obtained by Neville Stead from Cottingham South Junction signal box is no longer available in summer 1994. The trees on the right mark the former junction with the Newington branch, and although Ideal Standard's factory buildings remain, their private sidings (which were once shunted by their own petrol loco-motive) are abandoned and overgrown. An evening Hull-Bridlington 'Pacer' approaches. *N. E. Stead/CV*

WALTON STREET JUNCTION is where the Beverley line is joined by the spur installed by the LNER in 1924 to facilitate the running of Hull & Barnsley line passenger trains into Paragon station, thus permitting the closure to passengers of Cannon Street (see page 54). In September 1958 'K3' No 61923 brings a train from Scarborough over the junction.

By 1994 the H&B spur has been singled and is used only for crew familiarisation workings, occasional diversions and to enable light engines from the docks either to gain access to Paragon for the crews' 'personal needs breaks' or to clear, for other movements, the entire single-line section between Hessle Road Junction and King George Dock. The wooden fogman's hut survives as a Bridlington-Hull 'Pacer' passes and approaches Walton Street level crossings on 2 November 1994. Walton Street North and South are two of only four operating level crossings now left within the city out of the original 22. Since the demolition of Walton Street signal box in 1989 the crossings have been worked with the aid of closed-circuit television from Hessle Road box. The two crossings are together reputed to be the largest level crossing left on BR and were the first in the country to be controlled in conjunction with road traffic lights, from 1934. *B. Todd/CV*

WOODGATES LANE is where the Hull-Beverley line passes under the H&B high-level line leading from the western side of the city to the docks. 'B16/3' No 61468 heads a late afternoon Hull-Market Weighton-York service in May 1961, with Walton Street Junction in the distance.

Surprisingly both lines at this location are still in use and, by way of a contrast, Class '37' No 37235 works the Sunday afternoon Saltend Refinery-Mostyn tank train across the H&B line bridge on 8 May 1994. *B. Todd/RKH*

SPRINGBANK NORTH JUNCTION is slightly to the west of Woodgates Lane on the H&B high-level line, forming the northern extremity of the former Springbank triangle, and controlling the junction with the 1924 spur from Walton Street. On 18 September 1964, in the days when British-made cars were still being exported through Hull docks, Goole-based 'WD' No 90478 hauls an enormous train of at least a quarter mile in length past the box. The Newington branch (seen running at right angles under the train) had another eight months to live, and the crane in the distance is assisting in the construction of the flats visible in the modern picture. The bracket signal was taken down in 1968 and re-erected in the Normanton area.

The elevation of the 1964 picture is no longer available as Springbank North box is long gone, although some of the wooden piles that supported its rear down the embankment side can still be found lying in the undergrowth. An incoming empty tank train to Saltend passes the site behind Class '37' No 37689 on 19 October 1994. The line is now singled between Springbank South Junction and King George Dock. *Peter Rose/CV*

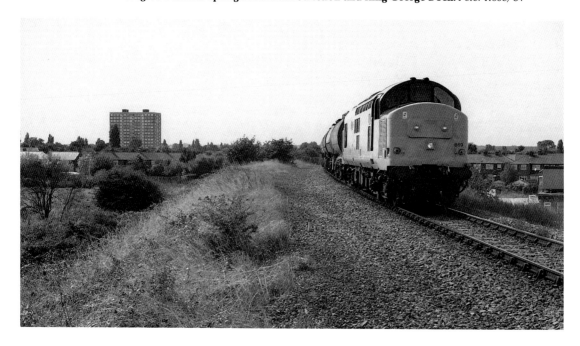

SPRINGBANK WEST JUNCTION was the western extremity of the Springbank triangle, where traffic could either continue in a north-easterly direction past Springbank North towards the docks or branch south past Springbank South and Boothferry Park to Hessle Road Junction. Springbank West also controlled the access to the large coal depot at Calvert Lane. On 18 September 1964 'B1' No 61032 *Stembok* has finished shunting Calvert Lane and is preparing to head south with local trip working J11.

The west to north-east leg of the triangle was lifted in early 1964 with the final abandonment of the H&B line westwards to Little Weighton. The box closed in November 1964, although Calvert Lane sidings and the associated west to south spur remained in occasional use until eventually lifted in December 1989. In December 1994 the site of Springbank West box can be found amongst the undergrowth on the left, while the house roofs on the right serve to identify the location. *Peter Rose/CV*

SPRINGBANK SOUTH JUNCTION box in the left distance is being passed by ex-North Eastern 'A7' 'Pacific' tank No 69781 on a short trip working in April 1955. The signal on the right controlled a long siding to the former H&B Dairycoates coal depot.

The former H&B high-level line is still double track at this point, although the signal box, signals and siding have long gone and been taken over by nature. The buildings on the right, however, remain as Class '37' No 37688 heads south with the Sunday afternoon Saltend-Mostyn tanks in May 1994. *J. F. Oxley/CV*

BOOTHFERRY PARK: Hull City is one of the few English football clubs honoured with its own station, a single-platform concrete structure alongside the ground appropriately named Boothferry Park and opened in 1951. In the 1950s anything up to eight trains would be run on match days. On 21 June 1963 'B1' No 61012 *Puku* passes with a short down trip working.

Hull City has never succeeded in breaking through into football's big time, usage of the station gradually declined and, although it still stands, it has not been used by football traffic since 1986. The line itself is now only used by docks traffic and Class '37' No 37689 passes with down empty tanks on 19 October 1994. Most local fans would agree that a ground admission charge of 3 shillings to watch the attractive Hull City side of the 1960s was better value than the £7 that it costs to watch today's team! *Peter Rose/CV*

DAIRYCOATES WEST (1): In 1915 the NER built steel girder bridge No 5A to carry the main line over the Hull central goods lines at Dairycoates West. On 16 April 1963 a special freight of sheeted highbar wagons bound for York via the Newington branch and Beverley and headed by 'WD' No 90695 comes off the St Andrews Dock branch and crosses the main goods lines, with bridge 5A behind.

Bridge 5A still carries the main line, but the only track now passing under it is the spur to Dairycoates East used by the Tilcon Aggregates train, as seen approaching behind Class '60' No 60002 on 2 September 1994. The train will run to Dairycoates East and propel back to the Tilcon terminal, to the left of the picture. No other rails now exist in this locality. *Peter Rose/CV*

DAIRYCOATES WEST (2): On the north side of bridge 5A (seen in the background) was the North branch link from Inward Yard. An unusual visitor to Hull, LNER 'O1' 2-8-0 No 63646 from Staveley depot, heads a trip freight, probably bound for Wilmington goods yard, on 19 April 1963.

Apart from the main line to the left, no trace of the railway remains at this location in August 1994. *Peter Rose/RKH*

INWARD YARD (1): The massive Inward Goods Yard, a hump-style marshalling yard, was opened by the LNER in 1935 and survived until closure in March 1974. The eastern section was used for the construction of a Freightliner terminal, which opened in 1969. It was not, however, successful, and closed just 18 years later in April 1987. Its short life was largely as a result of its location, which was very convenient for BR but unfortunately not for its major potential customers. Class '37' No 37067 prepares to depart with a westbound chemical tank train in 1981. Note the rail-mounted mobile crane.

Apart from the single track in the background used by the Tilcon Aggregates service, the site is now just a few more of the country's thousands of acres of derelict railway-owned wasteland. Note the expanded factory and Hull City's floodlight pylons in the left distance. *A. Dibnah/CV*

INWARD YARD (2): The yard covered hundreds of acres and could accommodate more than 3,500 wagons. This is the view of the neat and tidy sidings looking west towards the hump on 22 July 1964. Diesel shunters of Classes '08' and '11' are prominent, together with 'B1' No 61176 making up a train.

Thirty years on this vast site is completely derelict and overgrown. The exact location of Peter Rose's picture cannot therefore be identified with certainty, but the Anlaby Park flats in the background (seen under construction in 1964) provide a link. *Peter Rose/CV*

VICTORIA CROSSING (1): Flat crossings were extremely rare on Britain's railways and this example, Victoria Crossing, a short distance outside Paragon station, was abandoned in October 1968 upon final closure of the former Victoria Dock, Hornsea and Withernsea lines west of Wilmington Junction. Through traffic from the West Riding bound for Hornsea and Withernsea used this route in order to avoid reversal at Paragon, a function performed today by the now little-used Anlaby Road curve installed in 1965, which enables through services to gain direct access to the Beverley-Bridlington-Scarborough line. 'B16/1' No 61452 clatters over the crossing with a troop special for Hornsea on 12 July 1959.

The 1994 view at the same location shows the abandoned trackbed crossing the existing Beverley line with St Matthew's Church still dominating the background. *N. E. Stead/CV*

VICTORIA CROSSING (2): This view from the south-west side of Victoria Crossing shows 'WD' No 90352 working empty chalk wagons from Wilmington to Hessle Quarry on 10 March 1967. Nine months later No 90352 made the final short journey to Draper's Neptune Street scrapyard where it was cut up on 2 January 1968, one of 201 engines of its type so dealt with by Drapers.

A BR lorry occupies the trackbed in summer 1994 as a Hull-Bridlington 'Pacer' crosses behind. *Doug Hardy/RKH*

BOTANIC GARDENS: Trains for the Victoria Dock, Hornsea and Withernsea branches (including those that had used the Victoria Crossing avoiding line) would pass through Botanic Gardens station and across another of Hull's infamous level crossings. On 6 February 1966 'WD' No 90478 heads under the footbridge at the station level crossing with Wilmington-Hessle Quarry chalk empties (see also page 6).

These lines were finally abandoned in October 1968, and the trackbed today is a derelict wilderness. The buildings on the left at the junction of Princes Avenue and Springbank West are just visible through the trees that have grown up. *Doug Hardy/CV*

PARK ROAD CROSSING was the next level crossing beyond Botanic Gardens, and is seen here being negotiated on 5 July 1958 by ex-Great Central 'A5' 'Pacific' tank No 69802 on a Sunday School special for Hornsea. A handful of these engines were allocated to Botanic Gardens depot, but all had been scrapped by early 1959.

Park Road is now a cul-de-sac at this point, but the trackbed is a public footpath and the crossing-keeper's house survives. *J. F. Sedgwick/RKH*

STEPNEY (1): The station in the early 1950s; a train is departing for Hull, with Park Road crossing in the distance. The picture was taken from the footbridge spanning yet another troublesome level crossing, this time with Beverley Road.

In 1994 the station building survives as a listed structure, along with the platforms and the trackbed, which is now a public footpath. Thanks are due to the landlord of the Station Hotel who kindly allowed the author access to his upstairs room in order to achieve similar elevation. *J. W. Armstrong/CV*

STEPNEY (2): Half a mile or so to the east of Stepney the line passed under the former H&B Cannon Street branch and crossed the Barmston Drain. A four-car Cravens DMU is bound for Withernsea on the last day of passenger service, 17 October 1964.

This location now has to be approached from the east as the bridge over the Drain has been removed, along with the H&B flyover. However, the brick bridge abutments can still be seen at both sides, as can the roofs of some of the buildings in the right-hand background. Sections of the H&B embankment also survive at either side of the former flyover. In autumn 1994 the trackbed at this point was designated by the local authority as part of an official itinerants' site. *D. P. Leckonby/CV*

WILMINGTON BRIDGE (1): The present Wilmington (or Sculcoates) swingbridge over the River Hull was opened in 1907 and replaced an earlier structure that had become a bottleneck as rail traffic increased in the early years of the century; it was designed to swing to allow the passage of river traffic. On 5 July 1958 it is being crossed by a Cravens DMU forming a Withernsea-Hull service.

Wilmington Bridge is now the property of Hull Corporation, and carries a public footpath. Much of the original NER drive mechanism and equipment also survives and the bridge is still occasionally swung for the river. The reason for survival could well be connected to the fact that the Act of Parliament authorising the bridge's construction stipulated that a public footpath must also be provided. *J. F. Sedgwick/RKH*

WILMINGTON BRIDGE (2): On 31 July 1955 BR Standard Class '3' No 77010 crosses the bridge and approaches Wilmington station with a non-stop special to Hornsea, formed as usual of a rake of vintage non-corridor stock. The long flat roof visible from above the third coach belongs to the former NER Sculcoates goods depot.

The same location in summer 1994 shows the bridge together with the goods depot, which, although currently derelict, is a listed structure. *J. F. Oxley/RKH*

SOUTHCOATES JUNCTION: just beyond Wilmington station was Wilmington Junction, where the Hornsea line parted company with the Victoria Dock and Withernsea branches; the latter two continued south-eastwards together as far as Southcoates, where they too diverged. An eight-car Cravens DMU set bound for Withernsea approaches Southcoates station in 1962 and crosses yet another of the level crossings, this time with the busy Holderness Road.

Of all the locations within the city boundary featured in this book, the transformation at Southcoates is probably the greatest, and by March 1994 there is no indication whatsoever that a railway ever existed here. The old buildings and shops have all vanished and the location is now a busy crossroads between Holderness Road and Mount Pleasant, a new outer ring road that occupies the trackbed. In order to obtain some elevation, it was necessary to stand on a ladder in the middle of the new road, much to the bewilderment of passing motorists. It was decided to perform this hazardous feat on a Sunday morning when traffic was not too heavy! *D. P. Leckonby/RKH*

89

DAIRYCOATES EAST JUNCTION: Back at the other end of the NER's Hull docks lines, 'J39' No 64947 passes a section of the shed buildings at Dairycoates East on a lengthy trip freight on 15 May 1959, bound for the eastern docks or goods depots.

As mentioned on page 76 the only rails surviving at this point in 1994 are the two tracks used as a headshunt and run-round loop by the Tilcon Aggregates service. In June 1994 Class '60' No 60010 approaches with the empty wagons prior to running round. While the buildings in the background were part of Dairycoates shed, they are not the same as those shown in the 1959 picture, which have been demolished. *N. E. Stead/RKH*

NEPTUNE STREET BRANCH (1): To the east of the previous picture the lines from Dairycoates to the docks were joined by the H&B line from Springbank South to Neptune Street goods depot. The pioneer BR Standard Class '3' No 77000 approaches the junction of the two lines on 17 February 1962 with a rake of empty mineral wagons bound for the docks. Note the distinctive fish-curing house on the right; only one of these once common buildings still survives, but it has recently been damaged by fire and, although listed, it will unfortunately have to be demolished.

The 1962 picture was taken from a road overbridge that connected West Dock Street with St Andrews and the Fish Docks at the other side of the extensive goods yards that formerly covered this area. By spring 1994 the Neptune Street branch has long gone, the road bridge has been demolished and the whole of the goods yard has been taken over by Clive Sullivan Way. A viewpoint from the grass banking between this road and the slip road leading up to it from Brighton Street shows (above the 'Portacabin' in the foreground) the two buildings behind No 77000. *D. P. Leckonby/CV*

NEPTUNE STREET BRANCH (2): On the same day as the previous picture, but looking in the opposite direction from the same bridge, Mr Leckonby took this evocative view of 'B1' No 61189 *Sir William Gray* working a loaded wood train out of Albert Dock in the distance on to the H&B Neptune Street branch. Note once again the distinctive chimneys of the fish-curing houses and the grounded wagon on the left, which appears to have been forgotten when the sidings to the north of the branch were lifted.

Clive Sullivan Way fills the scene in November 1994. The wall at the side of the road, which formerly led to the overbridge, and the building behind it remain to identify the location. *D. P. Leckonby/RKH*

WILLIAM WRIGHT DOCK (1): Between St Andrews and William Wright Docks the railway and docks road crossed, and in this view on 24 April 1964 'WD' No 90704 propels a load of vans over the road towards William Wright Dock. Some rails remain in the undergrowth in 1994, although they will never again carry a train, and the surrounding buildings and characteristic lamp standards also survive. *Peter Rose/RKH*

WILLIAM WRIGHT DOCK (2): It is estimated that in the heyday of Hull Docks there were some 300 miles of standard gauge railway in and around the complex. On 22 July 1963 'WD' No 90272 hauls a load of timber on bolster wagons off William Wright Dock. In the dry-dock immediately to the left is the trawler *Kingston Onyx*, and beyond that a tug.

It is difficult to appreciate that in 1994 the only rail connection of any kind to Hull Docks is via the almost entirely single H&B high-level line, which affords a limited access of just a few miles to King George Dock and Saltend Oil Refinery at the far eastern end of the complex. However, many of the former rail-served locations are readily identifiable today, as in this view of William Wright Dock in September 1994, including the capstan and wooden poles. The trawler visible in the left background is the *Arctic Corsair*, the sole survivor of the once common sidewinder trawlers, which is being restored as a museum-piece and will never put to sea again.
Peter Rose/CV

NEPTUNE STREET: On 26 July 1963 'WD' No 90099 heads west past Neptune Street signal box with a short freight bound for Withernsea, probably from English Street goods depot. Although Withernsea was to the east, there was no direct rail link from this point eastwards and the train would have to make a complete circuit of the city via the H&B Neptune Street and high-level lines in order to gain the Withernsea branch.

The area in summer 1994 is derelict, but shed number 27 still stands and its left-hand wall and roof apex may just be seen behind the Boyd Line office on the right. The towers of the distant Holy Trinity Church and the City Guildhall are also visible on the horizon. *Peter Rose/CV*

96

RIVERSIDE QUAY: Peter Rose entitles his photograph of Riverside Quay on 9 June 1961 'organised chaos'. A Danish bacon vessel discharges through the transit shed to the left and the covered vans being loaded will be bound for Manchester. Tractors rather than locomotives were used to shunt wagons in this area and one can be seen near the police officer in the centre foreground. Note how virtually all the lorries are of British manufacture, many from makers that no longer exist.

Words are unnecessary to describe the summer 1994 picture taken from the same walkway above the transit shed. *Peter Rose/CV*

KING GEORGE DOCK: On 10 October 1964 a railtour comprising a Birmingham DMU set visited a large part of the Hull docks system, much of which had rarely, if ever, carried a passenger train before. Here the train pauses for a photo-stop near King George Dock, at the eastern end of the complex.

This location is part of the sole remaining rail access to Hull docks. In August 1994 an empty tank train from Mostyn has arrived behind a Class '37', which has been replaced by Class '08' No 08605 for the tanks to be taken forward to Saltend Refinery. The roof of the former chapel on Hedon Road links the two pictures. *John Foreman/CV*

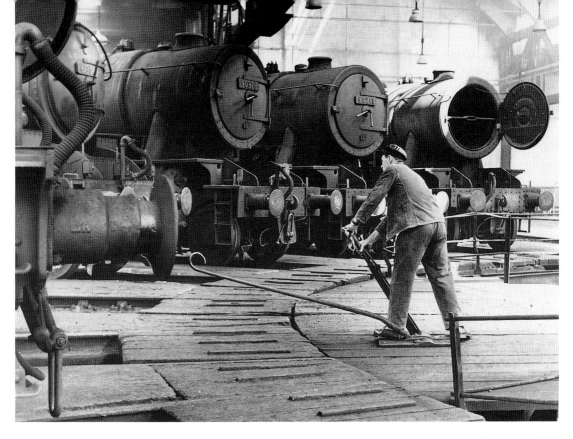

DAIRYCOATES MPD: There were four locomotive depots in Hull. Dairycoates was the largest shed on the NER, originally opened in 1863 and servicing mainly freight locomotives. It comprised two straight sheds and a roundhouse section containing six turntables. Part of the depot was extensively rebuilt in 1957 and this superb picture shows three 'WDs' and No 61306 grouped around one of the turntables in the new section. Dairycoates was coded 53A by BR until 1960 and 50B thereafter until closure in 1967.

The 1957 roundhouse still survives, in the ownership of Trans-European Port Services Ltd, who kindly allowed access for this picture to be taken. The structure of the arched roof, rear wall, windows and girders serves positively to identify the location, and elsewhere in the building the outline of the turntable pit can be seen in the concrete floor. *Hull Daily Mail/CV*

ALEXANDRA DOCK was the smallest of Hull's sheds, originally built by the H&B to accommodate the dock shunting engines. It was a wooden structure that had virtually collapsed by 1927, when its remains were demolished. No replacement building was ever provided and engines simply stood in the open air from then until official closure in the mid-1960s. Here is the 'shed' in late 1952 with ex-North Eastern 'J72' 0-6-0T No 68676, BR-built version No 69001 and another unidentified example, and 'J77' 0-6-0T Nos 68429, 68435 and 68413. Note the imposing vessel in the graving (dry) dock behind.

Apart from the removal of the rails the site is virtually unchanged in August 1994, and the graving dock is still in use. The embankment and buildings are soon, however, to be flattened. *N. E. Stead/RKH*

SPRINGHEAD MPD: The H&B's main depot and works were at Springhead, about a mile to the west of the Springbank triangle. Springhead was the parent depot to Alexandra Dock and provided the majority of the dock shunters. By the early 1950s, when Jack Armstrong took this picture of No 69001 and a number of her sisters, the building had already become dilapidated, and the shed closed to steam in December 1958, although it continued to be used for storage and to maintain diesel locomotives and units until July 1961. Springhead was coded 53C by BR.

The whole of the extensive Springhead shed and works site lay derelict for many years but has now been developed for housing. The exact location was meticulously plotted by the authors using large-scale OS maps and scale rules, and they challenge anybody who disagrees to prove them wrong! *J. W. Armstrong/CV*

BOTANIC GARDENS MPD: The NER shed at Botanic Gardens was opened in 1901 and was the principal passenger locomotive shed for Hull, being the nearest to Paragon. On 17 August 1958 'G5' No 67280 (strangely bearing a Leeds Copley Hill shedplate) and 'A5' No 69811 simmer outside the steam shed. It closed to steam in June 1959 and became a DMU maintenance depot. Coded 53B until 1960, it was 50C thereafter.

By March 1993 most of the shed buildings have been demolished, as the depot is now only used for refuelling and very minor maintenance, although it still possesses a turntable. The wall is not the one in the 1958 picture, which stood along the line of rubble beyond the track in the foreground. *G. W. Morrison/CV*

VICTORIA PIER: A good question for any railway trivia quiz is 'Name the railway station that from the day it opened in 1880 until the day it closed in 1981 never had a train in it'. The answer is the Hull Corporation Victoria Pier station where passengers bought tickets to travel on the railway-operated ferry across the Humber to New Holland. The Manchester, Sheffield & Lincolnshire Railway (later the Great Central) had possessed rights of access into Hull by this route since 1849 and in 1880 they erected this imposing building, which had all the usual offices and facilities of a railway station, except a railway. Here is the Pier Station frontage in October 1964; note the 'MSL 1880' trefoil inscription and the trolleys, which were used to transport luggage across the road to the landing pier.

    The building still survives as a listed structure, although it is boarded up and unoccupied. *H. C. Casserley/RKH*

The Holderness lines

The lines from Hull to Hornsea and Withernsea were opened in 1864 and 1853 respectively, and closed to passenger traffic under the Beeching plan in October 1964, although freight lingered on until April 1965. The majority of both trackbeds are now public footpaths.

SWINE: LMS Class '4' No 43078 runs through Swine station, on the Hornsea branch, in July 1955 with an empty stock train for Hornsea.

The station house still stands in the spring of 1994. Why get stuck in traffic jams when you can walk the 11 miles from Sutton (near Hull) to Hornsea? *J. F. Oxley/RKH*

ELLERBY: The first DMUs arrived in Hull in August 1956 and they replaced steam on the Holderness lines from January 1957. Thereafter the Cravens DMUs were part of the Hull scene for more than 25 years; here a two-car unit forming a Hull-Hornsea service calls at Ellerby (formerly Burton Constable) on the last day of service, 17 October 1964. From January 1960 the small intermediate stations on both branches became unstaffed, and tickets were issued on the train by the guard - a common enough practice these days, but quite innovative 30 years ago.

The road bridge from which the 1964 picture was taken has been filled in and the footpath diverted across the road, but the up platform edge is still visible. *D. P. Leckonby/RKH*

HORNSEA BRIDGE station was on an embankment on the outskirts of the town and was originally intended as the line's terminus. A Cravens DMU forming a Hornsea-bound train is seen in the early 1960s.

The view from the former station site in summer 1994 shows that the embankment is still in place at this point, and the rooftops to the left of the DMU are still visible. *W. B. Yeadon collection/RKH*

HORNSEA TOWN (1) on 2 August 1949 with ex-North Eastern 'A6' 'Pacific' tank No 69795 having arrived at the excursion platform with the 09.53 relief from Hull. Several of these cumbersome engines and their sisters, the 'A7s', ended their days at Hull in the mid-1950s.

Seen on the extreme left in early 1994 is the old main station building and station master's house (just out of shot to the left of the 1949 picture), which have been converted into flats and tastefully blended into a modern housing development occupying the remainder of the station site. The photographer's car stands at approximately the same spot as the 'A6'. *T. J. Edgington/RKH*

HORNSEA TOWN (2): Seen from the excursion platform LMS Class '4' No 43131 awaits departure from Hornsea with a Hull train in the mid-1950s. The train is formed of a modern engine with a motley collection of ancient stock, which was typical of the Holderness lines towards the end of steam.

At the same location in early 1994 the chimney stacks just to the right of the lamp-post are those of the former station building, which are visible above the second coach in the old view. *J. W. Armstrong/RKH*

HEDON: Turning now to the Withernsea branch, Cricklewood 'Black Five' 4-6-0 No 45238 passes the end of the single-line section and approaches the level crossing at Hedon station with a return excursion from Withernsea to Chesterfield, probably in the early 1960s. In July 1967 No 45238 made another journey to Hull when it became one of 732 BR steam locomotives (114 of which were 'Black Fives') to be cut up by Albert Draper & Son Ltd at their Sculcoates and Neptune Street scrapyards.

Housing development, trees and the local Gas Board have encroached at the same location in April 1994.
D. P. Leckonby/RKH

RYEHILL & BURSTWICK: The driver of an eight-car Cravens DMU set bound for Withernsea surrenders the single-line token at Ryehill & Burstwick not long before the end of passenger services in October 1964. While the Hornsea line was double-track throughout from 1900, the sections of the Withernsea branch between Hedon and Ryehill, and Ottringham and Winestead, remained single until the end.

By early 1994 the signal box has long gone, but the station house and heavily overgrown platforms survive.
D. P. Leckonby/RKH

OTTRINGHAM BAULK: Another eight-car DMU set bound for Withernsea and formed of Birmingham and Cravens units approaches the main road level crossing at Ottringham Baulk in May 1961.

The cottage is still inhabited in 1994, and as a bonus the lady of the house pointed out to the photographer that she has moved the wooden crossing-keeper's hut into her back garden, as seen in the third photograph. *J. F. Oxley/RKH (2)*

113

WINESTEAD, at the end of the single-line section from Ottringham, was closed to passengers in 1904. The driver of a six-car Cravens DMU forming a down train is about to surrender the token to the signalman on 5 July 1958.

The buildings on both sides of the line and even the remnants of the level crossing gates still survive in early 1994. *J. F. Sedgwick/RKH*

WITHERNSEA (1): 'V1' 2-6-2T No 67677 awaits departure from Withernsea with the 13.22 to Hull on 31 August 1956. A batch of these engines was transferred from the Middlesbrough area to Hull in 1955 in exchange for a number of 'L1' 2-6-4Ts.

The station buildings at Withernsea survive almost intact and the site is a thriving Sunday market. This view was taken from the same position in the summer of 1994, and the sight of the photographer up a ladder in the entrance to the busy car park caused a great deal of bewilderment to motorists and pedestrians alike!
H. C. Casserley/RKH

WITHERNSEA (2): 'L1' 2-6-4T No 67764 awaits departure from Withernsea with the 08.20 to Hull on 31 July 1949. The imposing building in the background is the one-time Station Hotel, which became a convalescent home in 1902 and later the Withernsea District Hospital.

The hospital is still open and the market is in full swing in early 1994. *T. J. Edgington/RKH*

WITHERNSEA (3): This delightful picture of Withernsea station on a bleak rainy day, probably in the early 1960s, speaks for itself!

The author has visited this location twice, both times in brilliant sunny weather, and it is rather a long way purposely to travel on a wet day! The former station building is now a fish and chip shop and is believed to be a listed structure. *Hull Daily Mail, courtesy M. Thompson/RKH*

The coast line and Bridlington

The Hull-Beverley-Driffield-Bridlington-Scarborough line was opened in 1846/47, and despite numerous attempts to close the section north of Bridlington it still survives. There is currently an excellent half-hourly service between Hull and Bridlington and hourly on to Scarborough, as well as a shuttle service to Beverley, which has never had a more intensive rail service than at the present time. The line through Market Weighton to York (closed November 1965, see page 140) diverged at Beverley.

COTTINGHAM (1): This is the station on 26 September 1954, with LMS Class '3' 2-6-2T No 40057 propelling a Hull-Beverley push-pull service. A handful of these undistinguished machines came to Hull in the early 1950s, but they were no more successful or popular than in their more natural surroundings and were soon sent back.

The view from the same station footbridge in spring 1994 shows a well-patronised Class '156' 'Sprinter' unit forming a Sunday Hull-Bridlington excursion. *J. F. Oxley/RKH*

COTTINGHAM (2): 'B16/3' No 61454 leaves the station with the heavy 11.50 Hull-Market Weighton-York parcels in March 1959. In the autumn of 1993 a 'Pacer' unit forms a Hull-Bridlington train at the same location. The photographer's car stands in for the Ford Popular. *B. Todd/RKH*

BEVERLEY (1): The interior of the fine North Eastern overall-roofed station in the 1950s; the roof had been renewed in 1908. Commentary on the 1994 picture is unnecessary - just spot the changes. *British Railways/RKH*

BEVERLEY (2): Standard Class '3' No 77012 stands at Beverley with the York-based North Eastern Railway Inspection Saloon in 1959. Little has changed in the intervening years as a 'Pacer' arrives at the station in May 1994. *N. E. Stead/RKH*

BEVERLEY (3): The RCTS 'East Midlander' railtour with 'D16/3' No 62571 in charge takes water at Beverley on 12 May 1957, while 37 years later, in May 1994, a Class '142' unit bound for Bridlington passes the same location. Note the tower of Beverley Minster in the background and, surprisingly, the same lamp pole as the one seen behind the cab of the 'D16'. *T. J. Edgington/RKH*

DRIFFIELD (1): 'B16/1' No 61469 passes Driffield Station Gates with a return Saturdays Only Scarborough-Blackburn train in 1954. Tony Ross returned to Driffield on 3 April 1994 to record the passage of the VSOE Pullman set headed by Class '47' No 47630. *Tony Ross (2)*

DRIFFIELD (2): Wansford crossing at Driffield on August Bank Holiday 1956; 'Crab' 2-6-0 No 42938 restarts a Normanton-Bridlington excursion from a signal check. The passengers, especially the children, must have had iron constitutions to travel so far in non-corridor coaches without so much as a toilet!

By January 1994 the signal box has gone but the warehouse and house remain as a 'Pacer' bound for Bridlington passes the crossing. Even 'Pacers' have toilets! *Tony Ross/RKH*

CARNABY: Dairycoates 'WD' No 90030 passes Carnaby with the 15.45 Bridlington-Hull freight on 16 April 1958.
Carnaby station closed in 1970, but the platforms and, surprisingly, the LNER gradient board on the left, remain in January 1994 as a Class '144' unit passes *en route* for Hull. Apart from the occasional engineers train and the annual visit of the weed-killer train, freight services on this line have long ceased. *Tony Ross/RKH*

BRIDLINGTON (1): Summer weekends at Bridlington in the 1950s were a train-watcher's paradise. Dozens of excursions would arrive from all over the North of England bringing a wide variety of 'foreign' as well as local motive power, every available siding would be full of coaches, and the shed (even long after its official closure) would be packed with engines. Here another incoming train is signalled as 'Crab' No 42762 from Manningham depot goes on shed after arriving with an excursion from Bradford (Forster Square) in 1954.

Although they are very rarely used these days, the carriage sidings surprisingly survive intact and the shunting signal has acquired a third arm. This view on 29 May 1994 shows an engineers train headed by Class '37' No 37684 in trouble with the fourth and fifth wagons derailed. *Tony Ross/CV*

BRIDLINGTON (2): An immaculate 'B1' from Mexborough depot, No 61165, leaves Bridlington past the South signal box and under the superb North Eastern gantry with a return Summer Saturday train to Rotherham Central in August 1955. Bridlington shed is in the right background and the spotters are filling their notebooks.

The magnificent 65-lever South box still survives in 1994, one of only four manual boxes still in use between Hull and Bridlington, although the semaphore signalling has been much reduced. The shed site is now a B&Q Superstore. Class '47' No 47630 leaves with the VSOE Pullman set on 3 April 1994. *Tony Ross/CV*

BRIDLINGTON (3): This view from the opposite side of the line shows the same gantry with 'B16/2' No 61421 piloting 'B16/3' No 61467 on a return excursion for Castleford on Whit Monday 1957. Double-heading in East Yorkshire was never common and the pairing of two 'B16' rebuilds was very unusual. The same location on 30 July 1994 finds Class '47' No 47762 working a return 'Pathfinder' railtour from Scarborough to Bristol. The track layout has been much simplified and loco-hauled trains are now few and far between. *Tony Ross/RKH*

131

BRIDLINGTON (4): 'K3' No 61941 arrives at platform 5 with the 12.22 Filey Holiday Camp-Manchester Exchange train on 5 September 1953. The place is alive with activity: passengers, porters, luggage and barrows.

Apart from the original 1846 platforms 1 and 2, Bridlington station survives largely intact and the architecture of 1911 vintage and standard of cleanliness is impressive. However, on the afternoon of Saturday 30 July

1994, the first weekend of the school summer holidays, platform 5 is virtually deserted. The most telling contrast is to the right of the pictures; where in 1953 there were rows of empty carriages waiting to form return excursions, in 1994 there is a bus park. A 'Pacer' arrives forming a Scarborough-Hull service. *Tony Ross/RKH*

BRIDLINGTON (5): The former overall-roofed section of Bridlington station (platforms 1 and 2) has been abandoned and sold off for housing development. All through trains now use platforms 4 and 5 and the terminating service from Hull, platform 6. An extremely rare pairing of two 'K3s' Nos, 61965 and 61932, both from Dairycoates depot, stand in platform 1 with the heavy 08.18 King's Cross-Filey Holiday Camp through Restaurant Car train in summer 1957.

The same viewpoint in early 1994 shows a Scarborough-bound 'Pacer' leaving platform 4 and entering the single-line section to Hunmanby, which the Hull train in platform 5 has just left. *Tony Ross/RKH*

BRIDLINGTON (6): 'B16/1' No 61456 passes Bridlington goods shed and crosses over into platform 4 with a relief train in the early 1950s; the entrance to the goods yard is on the right. In July 1994 the goods shed still stands, and Quay Crossing signal box beyond, as a Hull-Scarborough 'Pacer' negotiates the same crossover and enters the single-line section. *J. W. Armstrong/RKH*

135

BRIDLINGTON (7): Ex-Great Central 'J11' 0-6-0 No 64286 leaves Bridlington for Scarborough with a summer Saturday train from Manchester (London Road), Penistone, Barnsley and Pontefract in August 1953. Vintage 0-6-0s of this type and the more modern LMS '4Fs' were frequent sights on excursion traffic at this time.

The goods shed roof on the left establishes that the same viewpoint now is from the station car park, with the single line to Scarborough discreetly hidden behind a fence. *Tony Ross/RKH*

BRIDLINGTON (8): 'WD' No 90021 shunts the goods yard at the north end of Bridlington station in 1954. Forty years on this location is part of the station car park, with a new supermarket complex having taken over the site of the goods office. Very obligingly the contractors have left the imprint of the rails during their re-surfacing operations. *Tony Ross/RKH*

FLAMBOROUGH (1): 'B1' No 61305 climbs the 1 in 92 grade through the station with an express for Scarborough in August 1957.

Although Flamborough station closed in January 1970, both platforms still survive. On 30 July 1994 the photographer had to fight his way through a virtually impenetrable mass of brambles in order to obtain this picture of Class '47' No 47762 heading a rare loco-hauled train north of Bridlington, a 'Pathfinder' railtour from Bristol to Scarborough and return. *Tony Ross/RKH*

FLAMBOROUGH (2): An LMS Class '4' 2-6-0 propels an Inspection Saloon north from Flamborough in May 1956. The Saloon has been identified as the unique 1908 ex-LNWR vehicle now preserved on the Bluebell Railway.

'Pacers' are the order of the day in April 1994, the line has been singled and the goods yard is now a caravan park. The station house remains in the left background to identify the location. *Tony Ross/RKH*

The Wolds lines

By 1848 Market Weighton was the terminus of two lines, from York and Selby. Extensions to Beverley and Driffield were opened in 1865 and 1890 respectively, and the town remained an important railway crossroads until the complete closure of both routes in 1965. There was also the Malton and Driffield line, which opened in 1853 and was an early casualty, closing completely in October 1958.

WARTHILL: Although technically in North Yorkshire, Warthill has been included because in 1953 the level crossing there had the distinction of being the very first on BR to be fitted with lifting barriers, now so commonplace. 'B1' No 61122 negotiates the crossing with the 10.10 York-Market Weighton-Hull on 7 August 1957.
 At the site of the level crossing in spring 1994 lorries have taken over from the 'B1', but behind the photographer the station buildings have survived with the signal box ingeniously converted into a two-storey garage. *M. Mitchell/RKH*

POCKLINGTON: BR Standard Class '5' 4-6-0 No 73167 (then only four months old, despite its external appearance) waits to leave Pocklington with the 19.42 Hull-Market Weighton-York service on 1 August 1957.

Following the closure of the line in 1965 the station was taken over by Pocklington School, the ends bricked up, and it was converted into a gymnasium and recreation centre, thus ensuring the survival of the fine York & North Midland Railway overall roof and impressive colonnade outside the main entrance. All that is missing in spring 1994 is the track and signalling. *M. Mitchell/RKH*

142

MARKET WEIGHTON (1): The preserved Gresley 'K4' 2-6-0 No 3442 *The Great Marquess* and the now-preserved 'K1' 2-6-0 No 62005 double-head the 'Whitby Moors Rail Tour' past Market Weighton East signal box on 6 March 1965, bound for Driffield, Bridlington, Scarborough, Whitby and Pickering. Apart from the trackbed, now a public footpath, nothing whatsoever survives in the winter of 1993 to indicate that a railway ever existed at this point.
G. W. Morrison/RKH

MARKET WEIGHTON (2): 'B1' No 61276 leaves Market Weighton with a Bridlington (via Driffield) train in 1954; note the neatly tended border and shrubs.

Again, apart from the trackbed to the east and one pair of gate posts at the end of the former access road, nothing whatsoever remains of the busy station complex at Market Weighton. The station site is a local authority housing development, the goods shed has long gone and the impressive station building visible over the third, fourth and fifth coaches of the train was demolished in the 1970s following an argument with a lorry. *Tony Ross/RKH*

MARKET WEIGHTON (3): The view from Market Weighton East box of the junction of the Driffield and Beverley lines in the summer of 1961. 'B1' No 61084, a York resident for most of its life, negotiates the junction with a returning relief from Bridlington to Leeds.

In early 1994 the diverging trackbeds are still apparent, along with the public footpath that crossed the line at this point. It is possible to walk both trackbeds, either straight on along what is now Hudsons Way to Beverley or to the left up the 4 miles of 1 in 95/100 climb to Enthorpe. *N. E. Stead/RKH*

CHERRY BURTON: Class '40' No D282 heads a York-Market Weighton-Hull train through Cherry Burton station on 12 June 1965, a few months before closure of the line.

Although Cherry Burton closed to passengers as early as January 1959, it is still remarkably intact in the spring of 1994, and it was possible to obtain the comparative view by standing on exactly the same section of wall as had Mr Leckonby 29 years earlier. *D. P. Leckonby/RKH*

DUFFIELD: With the exception of Market Weighton, all the intermediate stations between Selby and Driffield had closed by September 1954. The real value of this cross-country line was as a through route from the West Riding to the Yorkshire coast, avoiding York and Hull. Duffield Gate station had closed as long ago as 1890, and 'B16/1' No 61471 blasts past the former station buildings with the 08.30 Manchester Exchange-Filey Holiday Camp on 25 August 1956.

In August 1994 the remote station house is still occupied, but everything else is undergrowth and green fields. *J. F. Sedgwick/RKH*

HIGH FIELD (1): The village of Bubwith boasted two stations within a mile of each other; one was Bubwith itself, which was near to the village centre, and the other was High Field, where 'K3' No 61899 is seen passing the staggered up platform with the 09.50 Sowerby Bridge-Scarborough train on 25 August 1956.

As with many others in the area, this redundant trackbed is now a local authority-maintained public footpath and nature trail, as seen from the same viewpoint in December 1992. *J. F. Sedgwick/RKH*

HIGH FIELD (2) looking east on the same day in 1956 and showing the staggered down platform. 'B16/3' No 61454 runs through with the 10.15 Scarborough (Londesborough Road)-Manchester (London Road) train.

Having lain derelict for many years, the station house is occupied by December 1992 and the platform survives, although hidden by undergrowth. In the two years since this picture was taken the conifer trees have grown to the extent that they now almost obscure the house from this viewpoint. *J. F. Sedgwick/RKH*

EVERINGHAM: An evocative picture of the station on 25 August 1956 showing one of the last survivors of the graceful ex-North Eastern 'R' Class 4-4-0s, No 62395 of Selby depot, piloting LMS Class '4' No 43123 on the 11.10 (Saturdays only) Scarborough-Liverpool Exchange.

The platforms survive in December 1992, but what a pity an example of an 'R' Class locomotive does not. *J. F. Sedgwick/RKH*

NEAR ENTHORPE: From Market Weighton East, down trains faced a testing 4-mile climb at 1 in 95/100 to Enthorpe. It is possible to walk this section today and still to find large chunks of clinker amongst the ballast as poignant reminders of exasperated firemen and steam-shy 'B16s' from 40 years before. In this unusual picture taken from the Goodmanham to Middleton-on-the-Wolds road, the 'K4' and 'K1' head the 'Whitby Moors Rail Tour' (see pages 142-3) up the bank on 6 March 1965.

A line of trees marks the trackbed in April 1994, and the surrounding landscape is totally unchanged.
J. Spencer Gilks/RKH

ENTHORPE CUTTING: One can only wonder at the determination and skill of the men who had to excavate the massive chalk cutting at Enthorpe more than 100 years ago with little more than picks, shovels and horses to help them. 'D49/2' No 62770 *The Puckeridge* and LMS Class '4' No 43057 (both from Selby depot) approach the summit of the climb with a Sowerby Bridge-Scarborough train on 22 August 1959.

By the summer of 1994 Enthorpe cutting is more overgrown and some of the chalk has slipped on to the trackbed, but the bulk of the earthworks remain as a testimony to the Victorian engineers. *N. E. Stead/RKH*

ENTHORPE was the summit of a longer but slightly easier climb from the east, and 'B16/1' No 61414 passes the closed station with a Filey-Manchester train on 22 August 1959.

In the summer of 1994 the original station buildings have gone but the platforms remain, as does one of the concrete supports for the station nameboard and a lamp standard. The site and the station house are now privately owned and thanks are due to the owners for allowing access. *N. E. Stead/RKH*

MIDDLETON-ON-THE-WOLDS station closed in September 1954, and here are the remains on 25 August 1956 with 'B16/1' No 61459 blasting through with the 14.57 (Saturdays only) Scarborough (Londesborough Road)-Derby train.

The platforms, buildings and signal box have completely vanished, although there remains in the undergrowth on the right sections of the characteristic fencing and the concrete lamp standard. The photographer's wife Jean stands opposite this in early 1993 on the same spot as the 'B16' 37 years earlier. *J. F. Sedgwick/RKH*

GARTON station on the Driffield-Malton section was photographed on 25 September 1958, with Malton-based 'J39' No 64928 working the twice-weekly 10.10 pick-up freight from Malton to Market Weighton and Selby about a month before complete closure of the line.

The station buildings and yard are now occupied by a scrap vehicle dealer and guarded by a ferocious dog. Fortunately for the photographer he arrived to take this picture in the summer of 1994 just before the proprietors closed up for the day and released the animal - thanks to them for allowing access. *Tony Ross/RKH*

FIMBER ROAD level crossing in September 1957 being negotiated by ex-North Eastern 'J27' 0-6-0 No 65849 working the 10.10 pick-up freight. Apart from the gate house there is nothing left in 1994 to indicate that a railway ever ran here. *Tony Ross/RKH*

SLEDMERE & FIMBER: Shortly before the previous picture was taken, No 65849 shunts the yard at Sledmere & Fimber. In its heyday this remote station was patronised by Royalty visiting nearby Sledmere House.

By April 1994 the site has been converted into a pleasant picnic area and can be positively identified from the background hills and line of trees, all the buildings having been demolished. A closer inspection of the site also reveals the three different levels shown in the 1957 picture, namely the track behind the hut on the far right, the stone platform and dock in the centre of the picture and of course the ground level. *Tony Ross/RKH*

INDEX OF LOCATIONS